Basic Shaft Alignment Workbook

Fifth Edition

Text, illustrations, and photographs by John Piotrowski

Dedicated to Bobbie Jo, Tracy, Paula, Peter, Magdalena, Joseph, Robert, Betty and the many people who struggle with this problem on a day to day basis and receive no recognition for a job well done.

www.turvac.com

Preface

Welcome to the introductory book on shaft alignment of rotating machinery! The purpose of this book is to give the beginning student an overview of the basic topics in shaft alignment. It starts by explaining why shaft alignment is important on rotating machinery. It then discusses the types of misalignment conditions, provides a clear definition of shaft misalignment, and explains how to determine acceptable alignment tolerances. How to align rotating machinery is then covered in a step by step procedure. Several important preliminary steps are explained to prevent problems during the alignment process and reduce operational problems with the machinery. The Workbook then reviews three different alignment measurement methods and their associated alignment modeling techniques providing concise, rational solutions for efficient alignment corrections.

This Workbook is primarily used as a training guide for people attending shaft alignment training courses and then, hopefully as a field guide for the trades person, technician, foreman, and engineer doing machinery alignment in the field. I have tried to keep the text to a minimum and portray as many of the alignment procedures and techniques in illustrations as much as possible.

Shaft alignment looks deceptively simple to do but in reality, it is a struggle between you and the machine. By applying a little bit of intelligence, patience, and perseverance, usually everything straightens out in the long run. Best of luck to all of you who are willing to give this a try!

Table of Contents

Shaft Alignment Modeling Techniques   52

Shaft Alignment Modeling Techniques   58

Positioning the Machinery   62

Index   68

The Importance of Shaft Alignment

The most frequently asked questions by managers, engineers, foremen, contractors, and trades people concerning the subject of shaft misalignment and its importance in maintaining industrial rotating machinery are discussed. The first part of this workbook will review what shaft misalignment is, a brief summary of the alignment procedure, why the quality of alignment needs to be improved, the consequences of misaligned machinery, and the frequency that alignment should be checked.

What exactly is shaft misalignment?

In very broad terms, shaft misalignment occurs when the centerlines of rotation of two or more machinery shafts are not in line with each other. As simple as that may sound, there still exists a considerable amount of confusion to people who are just beginning to study this subject when trying to precisely define the amount of misalignment that may exist between two shafts flexibly or rigidly coupled together.

How accurate does the alignment have to be? How do you measure misalignment when there are so many different coupling designs? Where should the misalignment be measured? Is it measured in terms of ... mils, degrees, millimeters of offset, arcseconds, radians? When should the alignment be measured ... when the machines are off-line or when they are running?

In more precise terms, shaft misalignment is the deviation of relative shaft position from a collinear axis of rotation measured at the points of power transmission when equipment is running at normal operating conditions. To better understand this definition, let's dissect each part of this statement to clearly illustrate what's involved.

The deviation of relative shaft position accounts for the measured difference between the actual centerline of rotation of one shaft and the projected centerline of rotation of the other shaft. Figure 1 shows a typical misalignment situation on a motor and a pump.

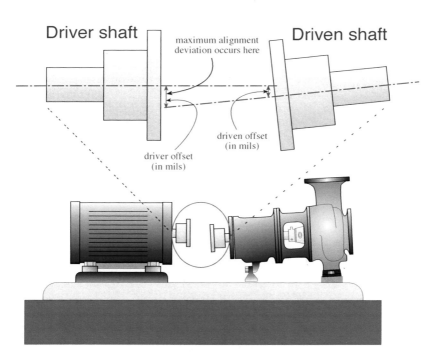

Figure 1. How misalignment is defined.

For a flexible coupling to accept both parallel and angular misalignment there must be at least two points where the coupling can "flex" or give to accommodate the misalignment condition. By projecting the axis of rotation of the motor shaft toward the pump shaft (and conversely the pump shaft rotational axis toward the motor shaft) there is a measurable deviation between the projected axes of rotation of each shaft and the actual shaft centerlines of each shaft where the power is being transmitted through the coupling from one flexing point to another. Since we measure misalignment in two different planes (vertical and horizontal) there will be four deviations that occur at each coupling. In the example shown, notice that there is a horizontal deviation and a vertical deviation at the point of power transmission on the motor and a horizontal deviation and a vertical deviation at the point of power transmission on the pump. The goal of the person doing the alignment is to position the machinery casings such that all of these deviations are below certain tolerance values. A tolerance guide is shown in figure 8 that will help in establishing a goal for the people who are doing the alignment.

The last part of the definition of shaft misalignment is probably the toughest to achieve and usually the one aspect of alignment that is most often ignored. When rotating equipment is started, the shafts will begin to move to another position. The most common cause of this movement is due to temperature changes that occur in the machinery casings and therefore this movement is commonly referred to as hot and cold alignment. These temperature changes are caused by friction in the bearings or by thermal changes that occur in the process liquids and gases. Movement of machinery may also be caused by process reaction moments in attached piping or counter-reactions due to the rotation of the rotor, something similar to the forces you feel when you try to move your arm around with a spinning gyroscope in your hand.

The goal of the person doing the alignment is to position the machinery casings such that all of these deviations are below certain tolerance values.

What is the objective of accurate alignment?

Simply stated, the objective of shaft alignment is to increase the operating life span of rotating machinery. To achieve this goal, machinery components that are most likely to fail must operate within their design limits. Since the components that are most likely to fail are the bearings, seals, coupling, and shafts, accurately aligned machinery will achieve the following results ...

- Reduce excessive axial and radial forces on the bearings to insure longer bearing life and rotor stability under dynamic operating conditions.

- Eliminate the possibility of shaft failure from cyclic fatigue.

- Minimize the amount of wear in the coupling components.

- Minimize the amount of shaft bending from the point of power transmission in the coupling to the coupling end bearing. Maintain proper internal rotor clearances.

- Lower vibration levels in machine casings, bearing housings, and rotors (*Note ... frequently, slight amounts of misalignment may actually decrease vibration levels in machinery so be cautious about relating vibration with misalignment).

What are the symptoms of misalignment?

Misalignment is not easy to detect on machinery that is running. The radial forces transmitted from shaft to shaft are typically static forces (unidirectional) and are difficult to measure externally. Disappointingly, there are no analyzers or sensors that you can place on the outside of a machine case to measure how much force is being applied to the bearings, shafts, or couplings. Consequently what we actually see are the secondary effects of these forces which exhibit many of the following symptoms:

- Premature bearing, seal, shaft, or coupling failures.

- Excessive radial and axial vibration. (*Note ... tests have shown that different coupling designs exhibit different types of vibration behavior. It appears that the vibration is caused by the mechanical action that occurs in the coupling as it rotates).

- High casing temperatures at or near the bearings or high

discharge oil temperatures.

- Excessive amount of oil leakage at the bearing seals.

- Loose foundation bolts (refer to "soft foot" later in this book).

- Loose or broken coupling bolts.

- The coupling is hot immediately after unit is shutdown. If it is an elastomeric type, look for rubber powder inside the coupling shroud.

- The shaft runout may have a tendency to increase after operating the equipment for some time.

- Similar pieces of equipment are vibrating less or seem to have a longer operating life.

- Unusually high number of coupling failures or they wear quickly.

- The shafts are breaking (or cracking) at or close to the inboard bearings or coupling hubs.

- Excessive amounts of grease (or oil) on the inside of the coupling guard.

What happens to rotating machinery when it's misaligned a little bit, or moderately, or even severely?

The drawing shown in figure 2 illustrates what happens to rotating machinery when its misaligned. Albeit, the misalignment condition shown here is quite exaggerated, but it serves to indicate that rotating machinery shafts will undergo distortion (bending) when vertical or lateral loads are transferred from shaft to shaft.

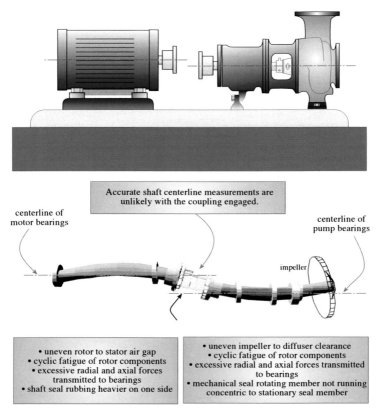

Figure 2. Rotor distortion caused by misalignment.

Please do not misinterpret the drawing! It is fully understood that flexible couplings do just what they are designed to do... they flex to accommodate slight misalignment. But the shafts are flexible too, and as the misalignment becomes more severe, the more the shafts begin to flex also. Keep in mind that the shafts are not permanently bent, they are just elastically bending as they undergo rotation.

Notice also that the pump shaft in this example is exerting a downward force on the inboard motor bearing as it tries to bring the motor shaft in line with its centerline of rotation. Conversely, the motor shaft is exerting an upward force on the inboard pump bearing as it tries to bring the pump shaft in line with its centerline of rotation. If the forces from shaft to shaft are great enough, the force vector on the outboard bearing of the motor may be in the upward direction and downward on the outboard bearing on the pump. Perhaps the reason why misaligned machinery may not vibrate excessively is due in part to the fact that these forces are acting in the same direction. Forces from imbalanced rotors for instance, will change their direction as the heavy spot is continually moving around as the shaft rotates, thus causing vibration (motion) to occur. Shaft misalignment forces do not move around, they usually act in one direction only.

The chart in figure 3 illustrates the estimated time to failure of a typical piece of rotating equipment based on varying alignment conditions. The term "failure" here implies a degradation of any critical component of the machine such as the seals, bearings, coupling, or rotors. The data in this graph was compiled from a large number of case histories where misalignment was found to be the root cause of the machinery failure.

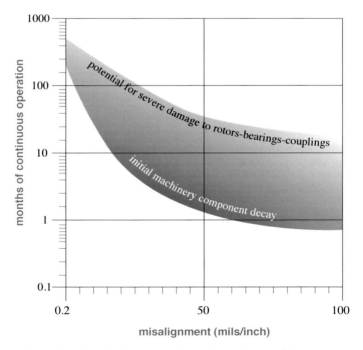

Figure 3. Estimated time to failure of rotating machinery due to misalignment.

How much time does it take to do each step in the alignment procedure?

There are eight basic steps in the overall alignment job.

1- Preparation - tools, people, training.

2- Obtain relevant information on the machine being aligned. Are there any special tools needed to measure the alignment or reposition the machines? Do the machines move from off-line to running conditions? If so, how much and ... do you have to purposely misalign them so they move into alignment when they're running?

3- Before you begin working on a machine remember ... Safety First! Tag and lock out the machinery.

4- Preliminary checks: runout, soft foot, coupling OK?, bearings OK?, foundation OK?, baseplate OK? Is the piping putting a strain on the machines?

5- Measure the shaft positions. Are they within acceptable alignment tolerances?

6- Decide who needs to be moved (which way and how much) and then physically reposition the machine(s) vertically, laterally and axially. After you've made a move, go back to step 5 and check to see that the machines really moved the way you hoped they did.

7- Install coupling and check for rotational freedom of drive train if possible. Install coupling guard.

8- Run and check the machinery.

Later on, we will examine each of these steps in greater detail but for now, let us look at the approximate amount of time it takes to perform each of these tasks to give you a feel for how much time this is going to take.

The graph in figure 4 shows the average amount of time taken to do steps 3 through 8. Step 1 is not on the graph since procuring all the necessary tools and training everybody who is involved can take a considerable amount of time to complete. As you can see, the two most time consuming tasks in the alignment process are ... performing the mechanical integrity checks and moving the machin-

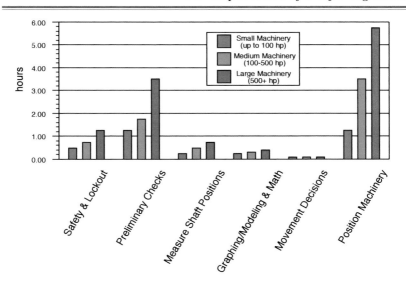

Figure 4. Estimated time to perform alignment procedures.

ery to align the shafts. It is not uncommon for accurate alignment to take from 3 to 8 hours, assuming everything goes just right!

How can I reduce the amount of time it takes to do alignment properly?

First, the people who are aligning the machinery have to know what they are doing and they have to have a goal to shoot for. They also require access to all of the tools needed to do the job and the tools must work properly. If your company purchased an expensive alignment measurement system that stays locked up in a cabinet, it is not doing anyone any good if they can not use it when they need it.

It is also important to have an alignment system that can provide you with alternative movement solutions when repositioning the machinery. The key to successfully aligning machinery comes from having the ability to arrive at a solution that is possible to perform and minimizes the required movement at the feet. Accurately calculating required movement at the machinery feet is useless if you can not move the machine the amount your alignment system is telling you.

9

How often should alignment be checked?

As previously mentioned, rotating machinery can move around immediately after it has been started. This is fairly rapid movement and the shafts eventually take a somewhat permanent position after the thermal and process conditions have stabilized (anywhere from 2 hours to a week in some cases). However there are slower, more subtle changes that occur over longer periods of time. Machinery will slowly change its position for the same reason your driveway buckles, or your building foundation cracks. Settling of base soils underneath the machinery will cause entire foundations to shift. As the foundations slowly move, attached piping now begins to pull and tug on the machinery cases causing the equipment to go out of alignment. Seasonal temperature changes also cause concrete, baseplates, piping, and conduit to expand and contract.

It is recommended that newly installed equipment be checked for any alignment changes anywhere from 3 to 6 months after operation has begun. Based on what you find during the first or second alignment checkup, tailor your alignment surveys to best suit the individual drive trains. On the average, shaft alignment on all equipment should be checked on an annual basis. Do not feel too embarrassed as you read this because you are definitely not the only person who has not checked your machinery since it has been installed.

How much money should I be spending on tools and training?

A good rule of thumb is to invest 1% of the total replacement cost of all your rotating machinery on alignment tools and training on an annual basis. For example, if you have 20 drive trains in your facility valued at $5000.00 each (total $100,000.00) then you should invest $1000.00 on alignment every year. This expenditure should only cover tools and training and should not encompass the time and materials required to do alignment jobs.

How do I know if the contractors I hired to install my machinery are doing the alignment properly?

Include some clause in your contract that requires them to provide you with the initial alignment data, soft foot conditions and the corrections made, shaft and coupling hub runout information, the final alignment data, the moves made on the machinery, and the final alignment tolerance. Ask if they have been certified in shaft alignment. Do not be satisfied with an answer like... "We used lasers and dial indicators." Dial indicators and lasers do not align machinery, people do.

Shaft Alignment Overview

- Types of misalignment conditions.
  - Defining misalignment.
- Determining alignment tolerances.
  - The eight steps of alignment.

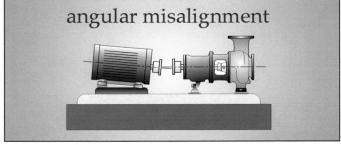

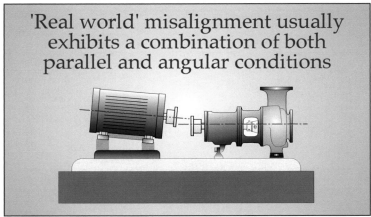

Figure 5. Types of misalignment conditions.

13

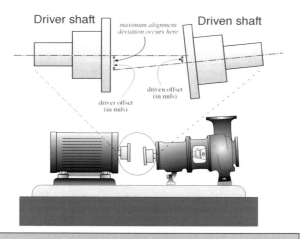

Driver shaft

maximum alignment deviation occurs here

Driven shaft

driven offset (in mils)

driver offset (in mils)

Misalignment is the deviation of relative shaft position from a collinear axis of rotation measured at the points of power transmission when equipment is running at normal operating conditions.

Figure 6. Defining misalignment.

How to determine the maximum misalignment deviation

Find the largest of the four deviations or gaps between the centerlines of rotation of both shafts at each point of power transmission (a.k.a. the coupling 'flex 'points') and then divide the largest deviation by the distance between these points.

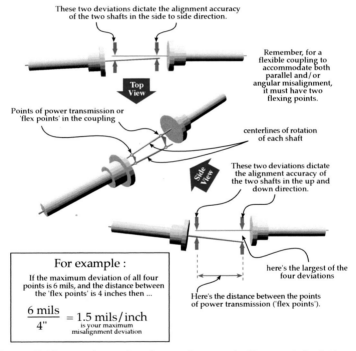

These two deviations dictate the alignment accuracy of the two shafts in the side to side direction.

Remember, for a flexible coupling to accommodate both parallel and/or angular misalignment, it must have two flexing points.

Points of power transmission or 'flex points' in the coupling

centerlines of rotation of each shaft

These two deviations dictate the alignment accuracy of the two shafts in the up and down direction.

here's the largest of the four deviations

Here's the distance between the points of power transmission ('flex points').

For example :

If the maximum deviation of all four points is 6 mils, and the distance between the 'flex points' is 4 inches then ...

$$\frac{6 \text{ mils}}{4"} = 1.5 \text{ mils/inch}$$
is your maximum misalignment deviation

Figure 7. How to determine the maximum misalignment deviation.

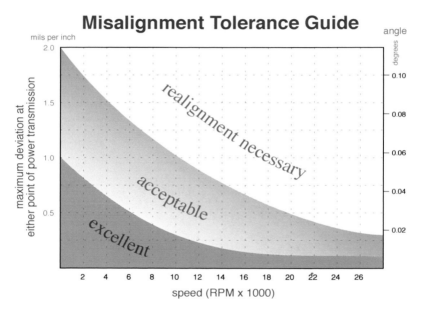

Figure 8. Misalignment tolerance guide.

The eight steps of shaft alignment

1 • Purchase or fabricate the necessary tools and measuring devices. Insure that the people involved in the alignment process have been adequately trained on: various alignment procedures and techniques, how to care for delicate measuring instruments and how to use them, what tools should be used to reposition the machinery, whether a machine is really ready to be aligned and operated or whether it should be removed and rebuilt, when a baseplate or foundation has deteriorated to the point where repairs are needed or corrections should be made, correcting problems that exist between the underside of the machine case and the points of contact on the baseplate, how to check for static and dynamic piping stress, what the desired off-line machinery positions should be, how to measure off-line to running machinery movement, what the alignment tolerance is for the machine they are working on, and how to keep records on what was done during the alignment job for future reference.

2 • Obtain relevant information on the equipment being aligned. Are there any special tools needed to measure the alignment or reposition the machines? Do the machines move from off-line to running conditions? If so, how much and do you have to purposely misalign them so they move into alignment when they're running?

3 • Before you begin working on any machinery remember ... Safety First! Properly tag and lock out the equipment and inform the proper people that you are working on the machine.

4 • Insure that you perform these preliminary checks: inspect the coupling for any damage or worn components, find and correct any problems with the foundation or baseplate, perform bearing clearance or looseness checks, measure shaft and/or coupling hub runout, find and correct any soft foot conditions, eliminate excessive piping or conduit stresses on the machines.

5 • Rough align the machinery and check that all of the foot bolts are tight. Then, accurately measure the shaft positions using measurement sensors such as dial indicators, laser-photodiodes, proximity probes, angular or optical encoders, or CCD's (charge couple devices). From this data, determine if

the machinery is within acceptable alignment tolerances. If so, go to step 7, if not go to step 6.

6 • If the machinery is not within adequate alignment tolerances ...

First, determine the current positions of the centerlines of rotation of all the machinery.

Then, observe any movement restrictions imposed on the machines or control points.

Next, decide which way and how much the machinery needs to be moved.

Finally, go ahead and physically reposition the machine(s) in the vertical, lateral, and axial directions.

After you have moved the machinery, be sure to recheck the alignment as described in step 5 to determine if the machines really moved the way you hoped they did. When the final desired alignment tolerance has been satisfied, record the final alignment position for future reference, the orientation of the soft foot shim corrections, and the final shim packs used to adjust the height of the machinery. If lateral and axial jackscrews exist, lightly "pinch" these screws against the sides of the machinery case, lock them in place, and make sure the foot bolts are secured.

7 • Install the coupling (assuming it was disassembled for inspection) and check for rotational freedom of drive train if possible. Install the coupling guard and make any final checks on the drive train prior to removing the safety tags.

8 • Operate the unit at normal conditions checking vibration levels, bearing temperatures and other pertinent operating parameters.

Before you start ...

- Dial indicator basics.
  - Check for runout.
    - Soft foot.

Dial Indicator Basics

bottom plunger type

back plunger type

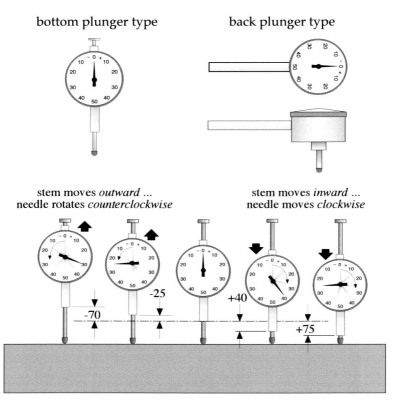

stem moves *outward* ...
needle rotates *counterclockwise*

stem moves *inward* ...
needle moves *clockwise*

-70

-25

+40

+75

Figure 9. Basic operation of dial indicators.

Checking shaft and/or coupling hub 'runout'

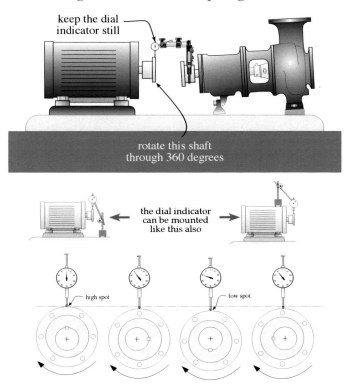

Runout checks are made to determine out of round conditions
(know as eccentricities) in the shaft or coupling hub.

Figure 10. Checking shaft and/or coupling hub runout.

Runout problems usually fall into one of these three catagories...

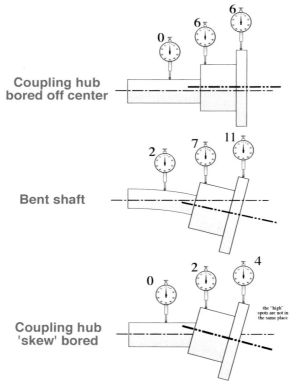

Figure 11. Runout problems usually fall into one of these three categories.

Recommended Runout Guidelines

shaft speed	maximum recommended Total Indicated Runout (T.I.R.)
0-1800 rpm	5 mils (0.005")
1800-3600 rpm	3 mils (0.003")
3600+ rpm	2 mils (0.002")

Figure 12. Recommended runout guidelines.

What is soft foot and why is it necessary to correct it?

Soft foot describes any condition where poor surface contact is being made between the underside of the machine casing feet and the points where those feet touch the baseplate or frame.

Quite often the underside of the "foot" and the baseplate contact area are not parallel and exhibit a very complex "wedge" type of condition. Other times the two surfaces are parallel but a gap exists somewhat similar to the short leg of a four legged chair. It is not uncommon to see three of the feet "toe up" and the fourth foot "toe down".

By ignoring this problem, tightening the bolts without correcting the soft foot condition will serve to distort the casing and put undue strain on the bearings and rotating element and cause a considerable amount of frustration when trying to align machinery.

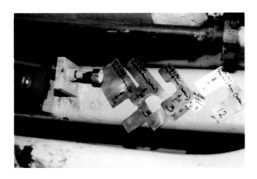

Measuring the gap conditions around all of the foot bolts

Step No. 1
Loosen all the foot bolts holding the machine case to the baseplate, frame, or foundation. Remove any dirt, rust, or old shim stock from underneath each of the feet. If necessary, use some sandpaper or emery paper (80 - 180 grit) to clean the surfaces on the underside of the machine 'foot' and the points of contact (sometimes called the 'pads') on the baseplate. 'Finger tighten' the bolts but do not tighten them securely.

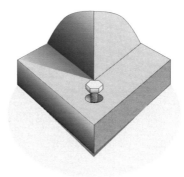

Figure 13. Soft foot step 1.

Measuring the gap conditions around all of the foot bolts

Step No. 2
Use a set of feeler gauges or a dial indicator to 'map' the soft foot condition as shown at the right. Determine where the contact is really being made and then record the gap between the underside of the machine casing and the baseplate around the contact area at each foot point.

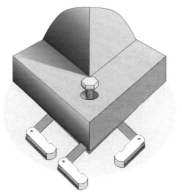

Figure 14. Soft foot step 2.

Correcting the 'soft foot' problem and verifying that it has been eliminated

Step No. 3
Eliminate the 'soft foot' by building a 'shim wedge' and installing the special wedges under each foot that needs correction.

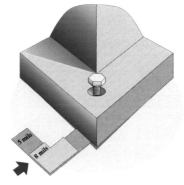

Figure 15. Soft foot step 3.

Correcting the soft foot problem and verifying that it has been eliminated

Step No. 4
Check all the foot points for lift with a dial indicator by ...
1 - tightening all the foot bolts
2 - zero a dial indicator on the topside of one corner near the foot bolt and then carefully loosen the bolt and watch the indicator for any movement
3 - retighten that bolt and move the dial indicator set-up to the next foot
4 - repeat the procedure at each of the feet recording the amount of lift at each foot

Note: None of the feet should rise more than 0.002" to 0.004". Once the soft foot shims have been installed, they should remain there for the rest of the alignment procedure.

Figure 16. Soft foot step 4.

25

Measuring the shaft positions

- • Rough alignment methods.
  - • Face-Rim.
  - • Reverse Indicator.
- • Shaft to Coupling Spool.
  - • Checking bracket sag.
- • Tips for getting good readings.

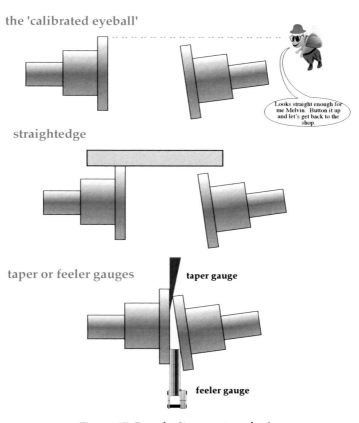

Figure 17. Rough alignment methods.

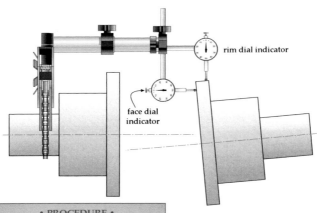

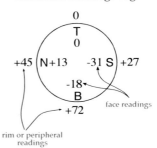

1- Attach the alignment bracket firmly to one shaft and position the indicator(s) on the face and diametral surface of the other shaft (or coupling hub).

2 - Zero the indicators at the 12 o'clock position.

3 - Slowly rotate the shaft and bracket arrangement through 90 degree intervals stopping at the 3, 6, and 9 o'clock positions. Record each reading (plus or minus).

4 - Return to the 12 o'clock position to see if the indicator(s) re-zero.

5 - Repeat steps 2 through 4 to verify the first set of readings.

indicator readings log

Figure 18. Face-Rim set up and procedure.

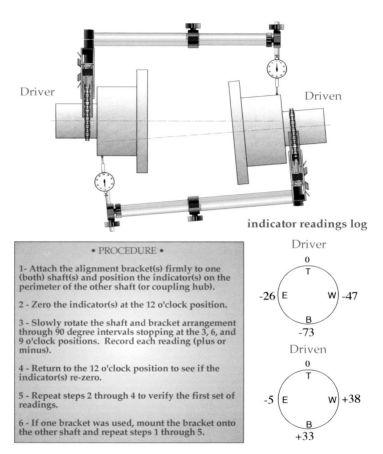

Driver

Driven

indicator readings log

• PROCEDURE •

1- Attach the alignment bracket(s) firmly to one (both) shaft(s) and position the indicator(s) on the perimeter of the other shaft (or coupling hub).

2 - Zero the indicator(s) at the 12 o'clock position.

3 - Slowly rotate the shaft and bracket arrangement through 90 degree intervals stopping at the 3, 6, and 9 o'clock positions. Record each reading (plus or minus).

4 - Return to the 12 o'clock position to see if the indicator(s) re-zero.

5 - Repeat steps 2 through 4 to verify the first set of readings.

6 - If one bracket was used, mount the bracket onto the other shaft and repeat steps 1 through 5.

Driver

0
T

-26 E   W -47

B
-73

Driven

0
T

-5 E   W +38

B
+33

Figure 19. Reverse Radial (aka Reverse Indicator) set up and procedure.

Driver

Driven

• PROCEDURE •

1- Attach the alignment bracket(s) firmly to one (both) shaft(s) and position the indicator(s) at some point along the coupling spool with the indicator(s) touching the outside diameter of the spool.

2 - Zero the indicator(s) at the 12 o'clock position.

3 - Slowly rotate the shaft and bracket arrangement through 90 degree intervals stopping at the 3, 6, and 9 o'clock positions. Record each reading (plus or minus).

4 - Return to the 12 o'clock position to see if the indicator(s) re-zero.

5 - Repeat steps 2 through 4 to verify the first set of readings.

6 - If one bracket was used, mount the bracket onto the other shaft and repeat steps 1 through 5.

indicator readings log

Driver to spool

0
T
+32 | E   W | +15
B
+47

Driven to spool

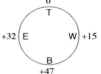

0
T
-8 | E   W | -31
B
-39

Figure 20. Shaft to coupling spool set up and procedure.

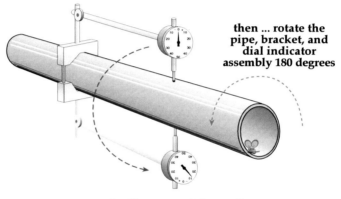

Figure 21. Checking and measuring bracket sag.

Validity Rule ...

(left) + (right) = bottom

The sum of the two measurements on both sides of zero should equal the measurement that is opposite of the zero within 10% of the highest value in the measurement set.

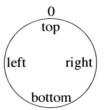

for example ...

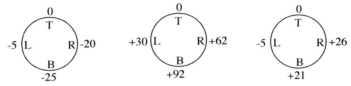

Figure 22. Validity Rule.

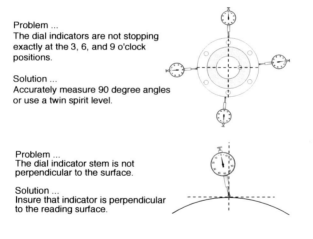

Problem ...
The dial indicators are not stopping exactly at the 3, 6, and 9 o'clock positions.

Solution ...
Accurately measure 90 degree angles or use a twin spirit level.

Problem ...
The dial indicator stem is not perpendicular to the surface.

Solution ...
Insure that indicator is perpendicular to the reading surface.

what the indicator path really 'sees'

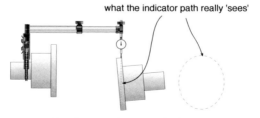

There's not much you can do about this.

Figure 23. Causes for deviations to the Validity Rule.

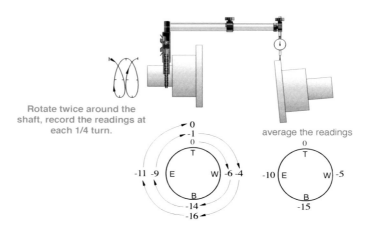

Rotate twice around the
shaft, record the readings at
each 1/4 turn.

average the readings

Figure 24. Suggestions for getting good readings.

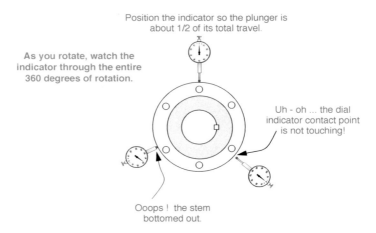

Position the indicator so the plunger is
about 1/2 of its total travel.

As you rotate, watch the
indicator through the entire
360 degrees of rotation.

Uh - oh ... the dial
indicator contact point
is not touching!

Ooops ! the stem
bottomed out.

Figure 25. Insure the measurement device stays within its range.

Shaft Alignment Modeling Techniques

Reverse Indicator Modeling Method

Scaling your drive system dimensions onto the graph paper

Measure the distances between the inboard and outboard feet on both machines, the distance from the inboard feet to the points where the dial indicator stems are touching the shafts, and the distance between the dial indicators.

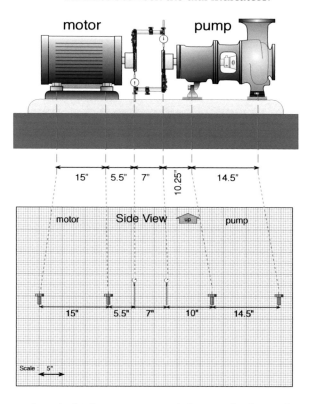

Accurately scale the distances measured above on the the graph paper.

Note: The scale can be 1″, 2″, 3″, 10″ per major division. Select the smallest scale factor that fits the entire drive system onto the graph paper.

Figure 26. Scaling your drive dimensions onto the graph paper.

35

Prepare two graph sheets, one for the Side View
and another for the Top View

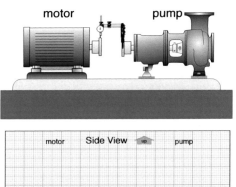

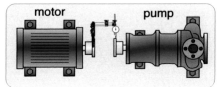

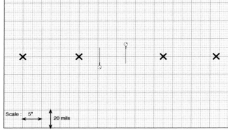

Note: This direction can be north, south, east, west, left, right, etc.

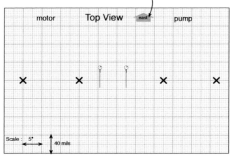

Figure 27. Prepare two graph sheets. One for the Side View and another for
the Top View.

When a dial indicator is zeroed on one side and sweeps through a 180 degree arc to the opposite side, the reading is TWICE the amount of actual offset of the centerline of rotation on the shaft being measured.

Side view of shafts

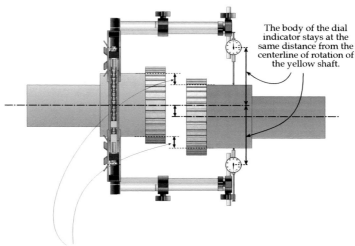

The body of the dial indicator stays at the same distance from the centerline of rotation of the yellow shaft.

The dial indicator measures both of these distances when it traverses from one side to the other.

Figure 28. Side view showing why reading is twice the actual amount of centerline offset.

When a dial indicator is zeroed on one side
and sweeps through a 180 degree arc to the
opposite side, the reading is TWICE the
amount of actual offset of the centerline of
rotation on the shaft being measured.

View looking down axis of rotation

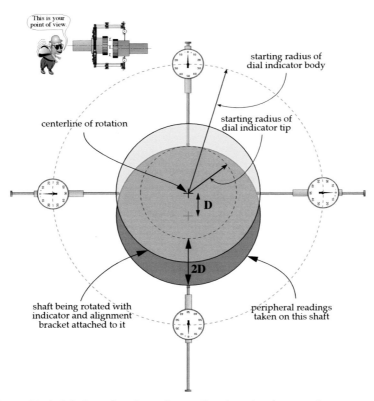

Figure 29. Axial view showing why reading is twice the actual amount of
centerline offset.

Cardinal Alignment Graphing and Modeling Rules

These rules apply when constructing machinery alignment models using any of the alignment measurement methods.

1. Only plot measurements that have been compensated for bracket sag.

2. Only plot half of a rim dial indicator reading.

3. Positive (+) dial indicator readings means the shaft is "low".

4. Negative (-) dial indicator readings means the shaft is "high".

5. Zero the indicator on the side that is pointing toward the top of the graph paper.

6. Whatever shaft the dial indicator is taking readings on is the shaft that you want to draw on the graph paper.

7. Superimpose your boundary conditions.

8. Select an alignment correction line (aka "overlay line" or "final desired alignment line") that is possible and easy to do.

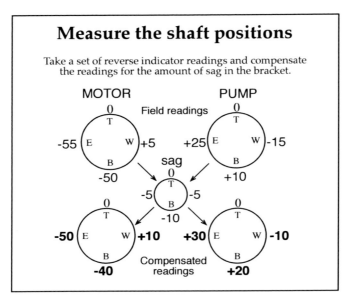

Figure 30. Compensating the field readings for bracket sag.

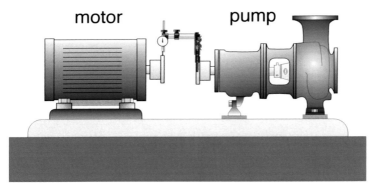

Figure 31. Measuring the motor shaft position.

When plotting the machinery shafts in the Side View, the only measurements you need to concentrate on are the readings you got on the top and bottom of the shafts. The side readings (north, south, east, west, etc.) will tell you where you are in the sideways direction so, forget about them for now.

If the bottom reading on the motor shaft was negative, start at the intersection of the graph paper centerline and the point where the dial indicator was taking measurements on the motor shaft. Mark a point above the graph paper centerline an amount equivalent to half the bottom reading. Draw the motor shaft centerline to go through the plotted point at the dial indicator position and the point where the graph centerline and the alignment bracket position line intersect.

If the bottom reading on the motor shaft was positive, start at the intersection of the graph paper centerline and the point where the dial indicator was taking measurements on the motor shaft. Mark a point below the graph paper centerline an amount equivalent to half the bottom reading. Draw the motor shaft centerline to go through the plotted point at the dial indicator position and the point where the graph centerline and the alignment bracket position line intersect.

Note: The scale factor from top to bottom on the graph can be 1, 2, 3, 5, 10, 20 mils (or larger) for each division. The idea is to select a scale factor that exaggerates the misalignment condition yet keep the entire length of the shaft you are constructing within the boundaries of the graph paper.

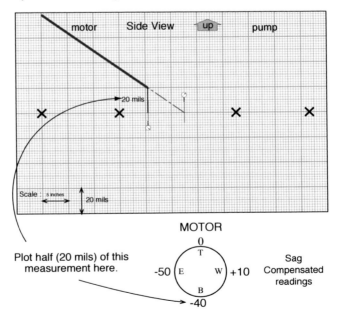

Figure 32. Plotting the motor shaft in the Side View.

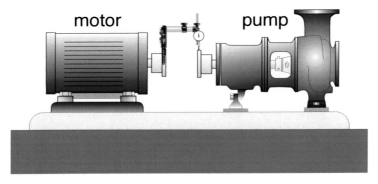

Figure 33. Measuring the pump shaft position.

If the bottom reading on the pump shaft was negative, start at the intersection of the graph paper centerline and the point where the dial indicator was taking measurements on the pump shaft. Mark a point above the graph paper centerline an amount equivalent to half the bottom reading. Draw the pump shaft centerline to go through the plotted point at the dial indicator position and the point where the graph centerline and the alignment bracket (now clamped to the motor shaft) position line intersect.

If the bottom reading on the pump shaft was positive, start at the intersection of the graph paper centerline and the point where the dial indicator was taking measurements on the pump shaft. Mark a point below the graph paper centerline an amount equivalent to half the bottom reading. Draw the pump shaft centerline to go through the plotted point at the dial indicator position and the point where the graph centerline and the alignment bracket position line intersect.

Note: It does not matter which shaft you plot on the graph paper first. Both shafts must be plotted before you can decide how to correct your misalignment condition. It is a good idea to draw the actual shafts as solid lines. The dashed lines in the drawing represent the imaginary centerlines of rotation of each shaft.

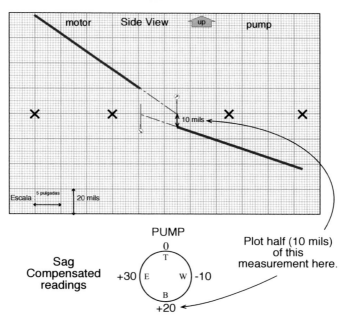

Figure 34. Plotting the pump shaft in the Side View.

The principles used to model the machinery shafts in the Top View are virtually identical to the way the shafts are plotted in the Side View as illustrated on the previous pages. The only element that changes is the viewing direction. As mentioned previously, one of the cardinal alignment modeling rules is "Zero the indicator on the side that is pointing toward the top of the graph paper."

Since you can easily become confused remembering how the machinery is oriented, it is recommended that you use compass directions (north, south, east, west) when recording your measurements. You can use any direction you want but stay consistent. Now that you are plotting the machinery shafts in the Top View, the only measurements you need to concentrate on are the readings you got on the two sides of the shafts (for example the readings on the east and west sides). The top and bottom readings have shown us where the shafts are in the vertical direction so, forget about them for now. Remember, you are now looking at your machinery from above.

There are two ways to zero the indicator on the side that is pointing toward the top of the graph paper. One way is to physically rotate the bracket and indicator over to the side that is pointing toward the top of the graph paper, zero the indicator there, then rotate 180 degrees to the other side and record the measurement. The other way is to zero the reading pointing toward the top of your graph paper mathematically and mathematically adjust the opposite reading the same amount.

The illustration in figure 35 shows a complete set of measurements on the top of the drawing with the indicator zeroed on top. For this example, if we want to zero the indicator on the east side (since that is the side pointing toward the top of the graph paper), we would change the sign of the east number and add it to both sides.

Complete set of Reverse Indicator measurements

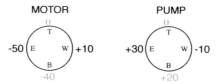

Mathematically adjusting the east reading so it is zero

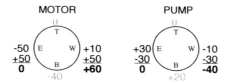

Here are the same readings if you zeroed on top and swept to the bottom then zeroed on the east side and swept directly to the west side

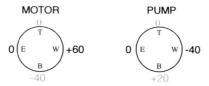

Here are the readings we need to plot the shafts in the Top View

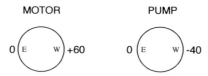

Figure 35. Zero the readings on one side.

45

If the side reading was negative, start at the intersection of the graph paper centerline and the point where the dial indicator was taking measurements on that shaft. Mark a point above the graph paper centerline an amount equivalent to half the side reading. Draw the shaft centerline to go through the plotted point at the dial indicator position and the point where the graph centerline and the alignment bracket position line intersect.

If the side reading was positive, start at the intersection of the graph paper centerline and the point where the dial indicator was taking measurements on that shaft. Mark a point below the graph paper centerline an amount equivalent to half the side reading. Draw the shaft centerline to go through the plotted point at the dial indicator position and the point where the graph centerline and the alignment bracket position line intersect.

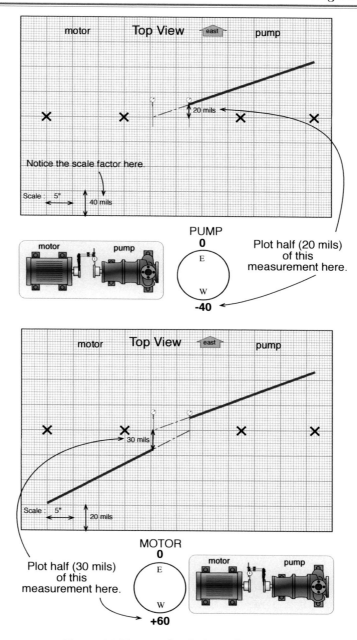

Figure 36. Plotting the shafts in the Top View.

Scaling the dimensions for asymmetric bracket arrangements

The ideal set up when using the Reverse Indicator method is to clamp the brackets and the dial indicators in exactly the same axial position on the shafts similar to the drawing in figure 26. Sometimes you may want (or be required to) clamp the brackets and place the dial indicators in different axial positions on the shafts as shown in figure 37. To increase the accuracy of the alignment model for asym-

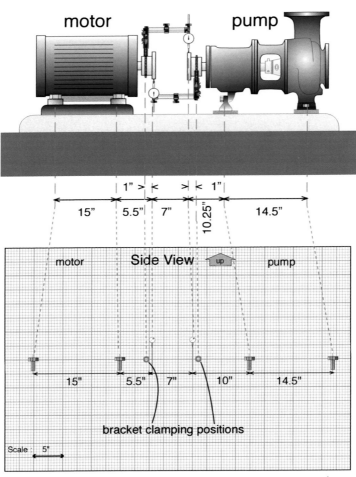

Figure 37. Scaling the dimensions for an asymmetric bracket arrangement.

metric bracket arrangements, you need to plot each shaft from the clamping positions through the associated measurement positions as shown in figure 38.

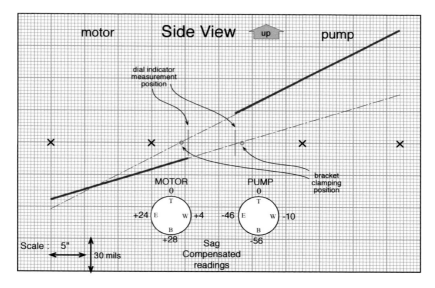

Figure 38. Plotting the shafts in the Side View.

Boundary conditions and the overlay line - How to effectively correct a misalignment condition

The major advantage of alignment modeling comes from the ability to superimpose additional information onto the model. In the Side View in figure 39, if we wanted to align the motor to the fan, we would have to lower the motor downward at the inboard and outboard feet. That would work if we had enough shim stock under those feet to lower the motor. But what if there are no shims under the motor and it was sitting directly on the baseplate? An alternative solution would be to construct an overlay line that connects the outboard feet on the motor and fan and then raise the inboard feet as shown in figure 39.

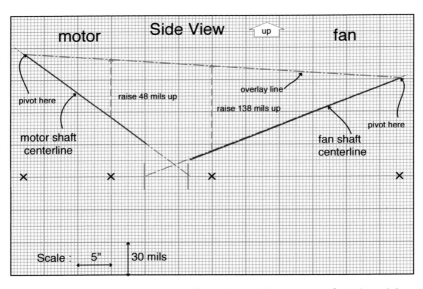

Figure 39. Overlay line connecting the outboard feet moving the inboard feet only.

You can also superimpose boundary conditions onto the alignment model. Figure 40 shows a Top View of a motor and a pump. The foot bolts were removed one by one and it was observed how far the inboard and outboard ends of both machines could be moved to the east and to the west before the machine would become bolt bound. We then plotted that information onto the alignment model to show us the east and west lateral movement restrictions then superimposed an overlay line to pivot at the inboard feet of the pump and attempt to center the motor in the east to west direction. The movement solutions at the inboard and outboard feet of the motor and outboard feet of the pump were calculated by counting the divisions between the overlay line and the actual shaft positions.

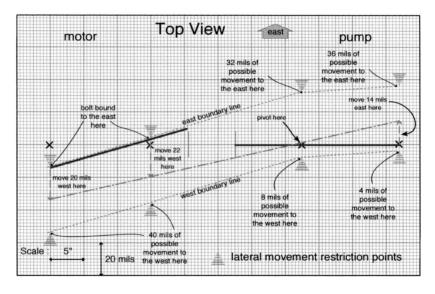

Figure 40. Applying boundary conditions.

51

Shaft Alignment Modeling Techniques

Face-Rim Modeling Method

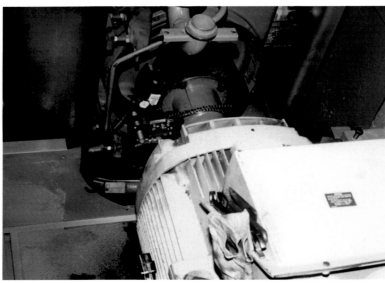

Measure the distances between the inboard and outboard feet on both machines, the distance from the inboard feet to the points where the dial indicator stems are touching the shaft, and the distance from the dial indicator(s) to the bracket clamping position. Accurately scale the distances measured on the graph paper.

Note: The scale can be 1″, 2″, 3″, 10″ (or larger if desired) per major division. Select the smallest scale factor that fits the entire drive system onto the graph paper.

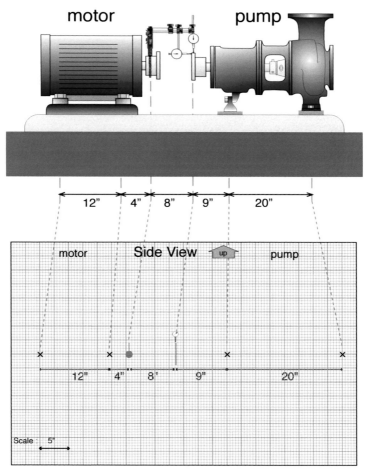

Figure 41. Scaling the critical dimensions onto the alignment model.

To graph the Face-peripheral method you need to have a clear piece of plastic with a T inked onto the plastic similar to what is shown in figure 42. The T bar overlay will represent the shaft where the dial indicators are capturing the readings. The shaft that the bracket is clamped to is the reference shaft and therefore will be drawn onto the graph paper centerline.

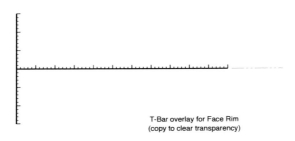

T-Bar overlay for Face Rim
(copy to clear transparency)

Figure 42. T bar overlay.

Scale the diameter of the face reading onto the T bar overlay as shown in figure 43 with the same scale factor used when scaling the machinery distances onto the graph paper in figure 41. The top part of the T represents the face of the shaft you are taking readings on and the base of the T represents the centerline of rotation of the shaft.

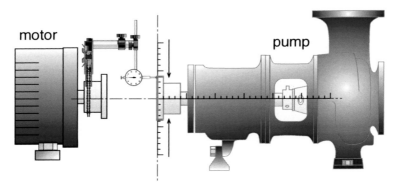

Figure 43. Top part of the T represents the face reading diameter.

54

In this method, you dual scale the graph. In other words, whatever scale factor you use from left to right to scale the dimensions along the length of the machinery, that same scale factor is used from top to bottom on the graph to scale the diameter the face readings were taken on when you transfer this dimension to the top of the T on the T bar overlay. Likewise, whatever scale factor you select to exaggerate the misalignment condition for the rim readings from top to bottom on the graph, that same scale factor is used from left to right on the graph when pitching / rotating the T bar overlay to reflect the face reading you observed. Insure that you use the same scale factor (inches) for both the machine dimensions and face diameter and the same scale factor (mils) for the rim and face measurements.

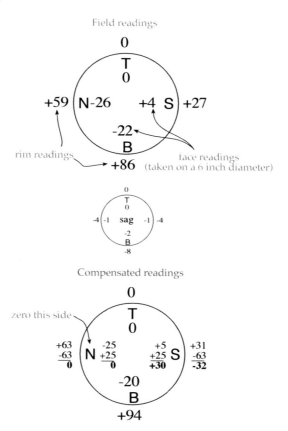

Figure 44. Compensating the field readings for bracket sag.

The Face and Rim method measures an offset and an angle of another shaft's centerline of rotation with respect to the line of sight of a reference shaft. The offset is measured by the rim indicator and the angle is measured by the face indicator. The shaft that has the bracket clamped to it is placed directly on the graph paper centerline as a reference and then the other shaft, represented by the T-Bar overlay, is positioned based on the dial indicator measurements obtained.

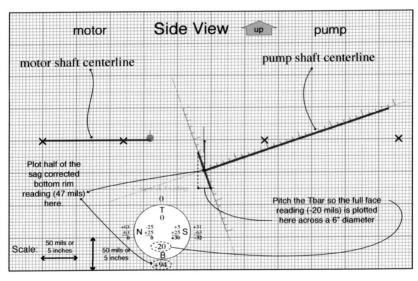

Figure 45. Plotting the shafts in the Side View.

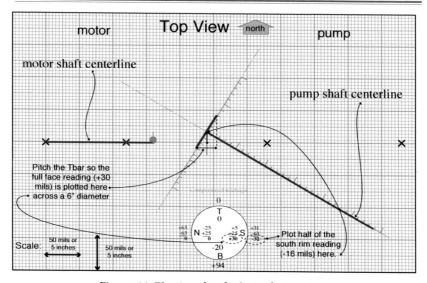

Figure 46. Plotting the shafts in the Top View.

57

Shaft Alignment Modeling Techniques

Shaft to Coupling Spool Modeling Method

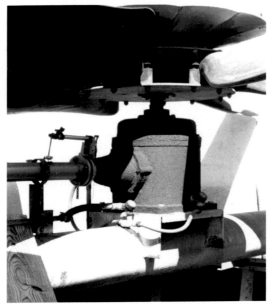

The basic measurement principle of the shaft to coupling spool technique lies in the ability to measure the angle between each shaft centerline and the centerline of the coupling spool (also known as a jackshaft or drive shaft). Since there is only one flex point at the end of each shaft, near perfect angular alignment exists between each shaft and the coupling spool. The coupling spool remains intact (connected to the shafts) during this procedure.

There are eight pieces of information that you need to properly construct the shaft positions using this technique:

1. The distance from the outboard to inboard feet (bolting planes) of the first machine.

2. The distance from the inboard bolting plane of the first machine to the flexing point between the shaft and the coupling spool on the first machine. Note that the point where the bracket is being clamped on the shaft is not relevant. A good distance to span past the flex point is anywhere from 3 to 24 inches. The greater this distance is, the more accurate this technique becomes.

3. The distance from the flexing point between the shaft and the coupling spool on the first machine and the point where the dial indicator is capturing the rim readings on the coupling spool.

4. The distance from where the dial indicator is capturing the rim readings on the coupling spool near the first machine to the point where the dial indicator is capturing the rim readings on the coupling spool near the second machine.

5. The distance from where the dial indicator is capturing the rim readings on the coupling spool near the second machine to the flexing point between the shaft and the coupling spool on the second machine. Note that this distance does not have to be the same distance as measured in No. 3 above.

6. The distance from the flexing point between the shaft and the coupling spool on the second machine to the inboard bolting plane of the second machine.

7. The distance from the outboard to inboard feet (bolting planes) of the second machine.

8. The eight dial indicator readings taken at the top, bottom, and both sides on the coupling spool after compensating for sag. Be aware of the fact that there will probably be two different sag amounts at each of the dial indicator locations if the distances were not the same from the flex points to where the dial indicator readings were taken.

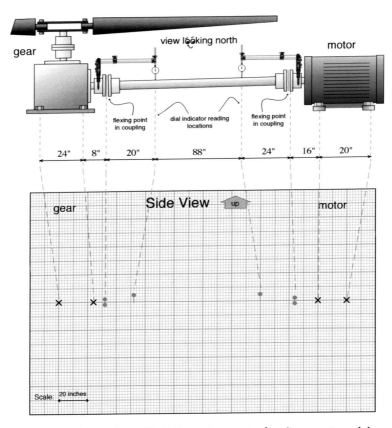

Figure 47. Scaling the critical dimensions onto the alignment model.

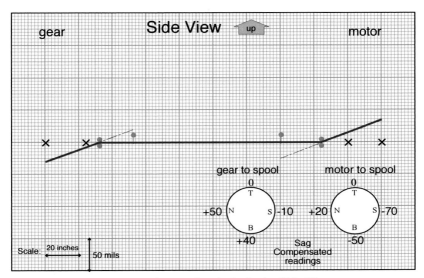

Figure 48. Plotting the shafts in the Side View.

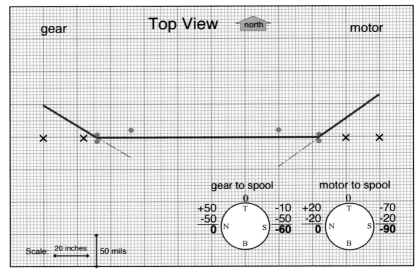

Figure 49. Plotting the shafts in the Top View.

Positioning the Machinery

- Shaft alignment in a 3 dimensional world.
- How far can the machines be moved laterally?
- Controlling your lateral moves.
- How to check for excessive static piping stresses.

Shaft alignment in a 3-dimensional world

axial position

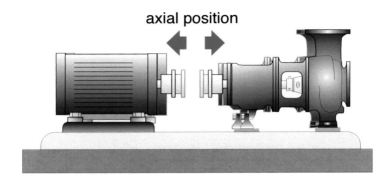

horizontal position

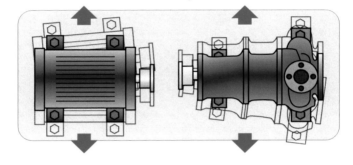

vertical position

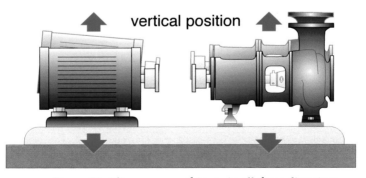

Figure 50. Align your machinery in all three directions.

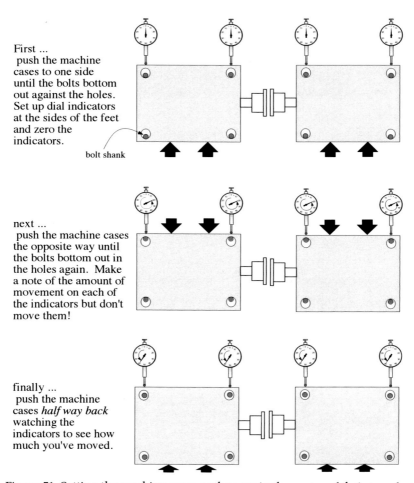

First ...
push the machine cases to one side until the bolts bottom out against the holes. Set up dial indicators at the sides of the feet and zero the indicators.

bolt shank

next ...
push the machine cases the opposite way until the bolts bottom out in the holes again. Make a note of the amount of movement on each of the indicators but don't move them!

finally ...
push the machine cases *half way back* watching the indicators to see how much you've moved.

Figure 51. Setting the machine cases so they are in the center of their travel.

Controlling your lateral moves

Machinery has a great tendency to misbehave when moving sideways. Quite often machine cases will translate or slide straight sideways rather than pivot at one end. For instance, if you are not watching what happens to the inboard end while you are moving the outboard end, a shift at the outboard end may have occurred that you did not notice.

Here are some suggestions to help minimize potential problems:

- Have indicators mounted to monitor any movement at the inboard and outboard ends of the machinery. Zero the indicators prior to loosening the foot bolts particularly with machinery that has piping or ductwork attached to it. If you see more than 2 mils of movement sideways on the machine case after loosening the bolts, you may have an uncorrected soft foot condition or excessive static piping stresses present.

- Use jackscrews wherever possible not only to move the machinery but also to hold one end in place when trying to position the other end.

- If you do not have jackscrews, use on of the foot bolts as a "pivot point", move the outboard end first, then use an alignment bracket and dial indicator to assist in positioning the inboard end as shown in figure 52.

First, loosen all but one of the inboard
bolts and move the outboard end the
amount you decided upon

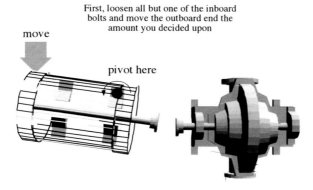

Next, tighten one of the outboard bolts, loosen the inboard bolt used
as a 'pivot' point, mount the bracket and indicator onto one of the
shafts, rotate the bracket/indicator over to one side, zero the indicator,
and rotate to the other side and make a note of the reading

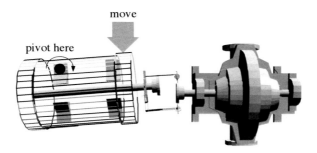

Finally, move the inboard end until the indicator is reading half of
the original value (assuming that you want the shafts to be collinear
when the units are off-line)

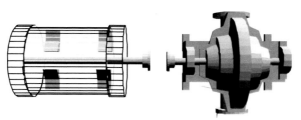

Figure 52. Move one end at a time.

Align the machinery and then attach brackets or clamps to one shaft and mount dial indicators in the vertical and horizontal position against the other shaft. Zero the indicators, loosen the foot bolts holding the piped machine in place and monitor the indicators for any movement. Ideally, less than 2 mils (0.002") of movement should occur on either indicator.

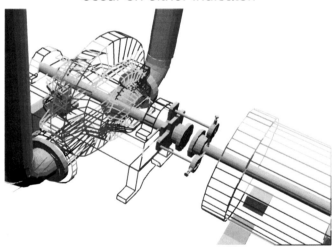

Figure 53. How to check for excessive static piping stresses.

Index

V